CHRISTIAN PERSPECTIVES ON ORIGINS

Steve Badger, PhD

Mike Tenneson, PhD

©2014

—Third Edition—
Expanded & Revised

Evangel University
1111 North Glenstone Avenue
Springfield, Missouri 65802
417.865.2815
www.evangel.edu

The authors have developed an Online Origins Survey.
For details, see page 48.

ISBN-13: 978-1500154745

ISBN-10: 1500154741

Table of Contents

Acknowledgements

Special thanks to the following people for their help in reviewing this material and providing criticism: Charlie Arsenault, Erica Harris, Bob Love, Gary Martindale, Bob Stallman, and Cindy Weiss.

Dr. Tenneson gratefully acknowledges a semester-long sabbatical granted by Evangel University that provided the time to devote to this research and writing.

Josh Tenneson did the cover art, and Andrew Breault assisted in printing.

Finally, any errors contained in this book are the fault of the authors, not of those who helped us.

Cover Art: Josh Tenneson
tennesonj@gmail.com

Foreword

Don't let the miniature size of this booklet fool you! Christian Perspectives on Origins is one of the most helpful and useful guides available for students and anyone else who wants to sort out all of the complex biblical, theological, and scientific issues surrounding this topic. It provides a wonderfully accessible introduction to many facets of the debate, often presenting various perspectives for consideration. This is an essential and much-needed approach, precisely since all too often advocates of the various views argue their positions as if that were the only plausible one. More importantly, this little booklet invites readers to reflect on their overall assumptions, their pre-commitments, and the implications of these aspects of their thinking. This in itself is an exceedingly valuable exercise for those of us who are attempting to love the Lord our God with all of our minds, as the Gospel writers have required us to do.

Equally significant to note is that the authors—Steve Badger and Mike Tenneson—are not only eminently qualified scientists but also Spirit-filled and fervent men of faith. They have committed their lives to working through these issues carefully and prayerfully considered how we might pursue answers to the many questions that remain. Along the way, they have already been a source of inspiration to an entire generation of students, opening up previously unseen vistas for learning that will ultimately bear the fruit of the Spirit and give glory to God. But their ministries have not been limited to the classroom and the science laboratory. Both are also ministers of the Gospel who have devoted their lives to serve the church, and they have played key roles in helping their fellow Pentecostal church leaders see the importance of providing a secure space for all people of faith to engage with these vital matters.

I have learned a great deal from Steve and Mike, and wished that my own college-age children could have sat under their tutelage. The next best thing would be for me to give this booklet to my children. I therefore recommend that all readers get an extra copy and give it to their teenage children or anyone else who is struggling to reconcile their Christian faith and modern science in terms of the origins of the world and of humanity. *Christian Perspectives on Origins* ought to be the first point of entry that will help all who read it with an open heart and open mind to take the next steps in their faith journey on this important topic.

Rev. Dr. Amos Yong, Professor of Missiology, Fuller Theological Seminary
Director, Center of Missiological Research, Pasadena, California

Preface

Why another book on Creation-Evolution? Our abiding love for the Lord and fervent confidence in the trustworthiness of the Bible bring us to the questions of Origins with a deep sense of reverence for the Creator. At the same time, we feel that God has used the divine gift of human intellect and science to bless humankind tremendously. God's power and divine nature are revealed both in the Scriptures and by His Creation (Romans 1:20).

Our purpose in this book is to describe the main issues involved in understanding the three major positions Christians hold regarding creation and evolution. We are not promoting any one of these common theories, but we hope this book will help you to understand your position better—and to understand better why some Christians embrace a different position.

Over the past ten years the authors have invested countless hours in reading books and articles on Origins. The authors invested even more time in discussing and debating the merits of what they read—sometimes agreeing, other times disagreeing.

At the beginning of our collaboration each of us held opinions with varying degrees of tenacity. But through this process of studying together, both of us have modified our positions—at least a little. We held different positions when we began, and we still do not agree on all points.

In our years of teaching science classes we've observed that the people who seem to have the least knowledge of the salient issues of the creation-evolution debate (and the larger issue of the interface of the natural sciences with Christian faith) are often the people who most vehemently argue that their position is the only biblical and orthodox position.

We wrote this booklet with Christian college students and faculty in mind. We hope that it provides the background a person needs to appreciate the complexity of the Origins debate and some guidance in avoiding the pitfalls so many other believers have stumbled into.

In this third edition, we have added a section on the inspiration of Scripture, more illustrative graphics, a section explaining in more detail the value of this booklet, and many other minor improvements. The list of sources and resources has been organized into groups, making it easier for you to find resources that fit your needs.

Beyond this, we have reorganized the text into six units: the Introduction is followed by units that explain the role of three disciplines in answering the questions of Origins: philosophy, theology, and the natural sciences. The last unit describes how people have attempted to integrate each of these three disciplines into a reasoned understanding of Origins.

In addition to a bibliography, we also provide our "Top Ten" list of books that we think provide a more complete and cogent presentation of the issues, evidences, and arguments that a person must grasp in order to form an opinion based on knowledge, rather than a dogma.

Steve Badger & Mike Tenneson
June 2011

Introduction

The Dynamic Tension

Ryan, a Pentecostal university student, is sitting in his biology professor's office. Dr. Price listens silently to Ryan. "I came to a Christian school because I didn't want my faith destroyed by godless professors teaching evolution. A creation scientist at our church told us that we can believe either the Bible or Darwin. Dr. Price, why do you use a textbook that presents evolution as *fact*? Can't you teach biology without evolution?"[1]

She thinks: How can I teach biology without weakening his faith in God and his confidence in the Bible? I cannot answer his questions in 30 minutes.

"My girlfriend, Courtney, is majoring in biology. She's a Christian, but she believes in evolution. My parents told me to stop dating her. My roommate's a geology major who thinks the earth is billions of years old! He rarely goes to church and often breaks school rules. I doubt he's really a Christian. My youth pastor warned me not to start down that 'slippery Darwinian slope.' He said, first you accept a universe that is billions of years old, then you start to think maybe God directed evolution and call yourself a 'theistic evolutionist.' Finally you become an atheist."

She thinks: I don't want to get in a fight with my literalist colleagues!

Ryan continues, "I don't want to know all the arguments and evidences for and against evolution. Just tell me what to think, what to believe.'"

She thinks: Many in our denomination reject theistic evolution. Some of our faculty hold different views, but I don't know what position our administrators take. I'm applying for tenure and promotion to full professor next year. If parents or pastors complain to the administration about my teaching, I might be passed over—or worse, they might not offer me a contract next year.

"Dr. Price, I'm so confused. Can real Christians believe in evolution?"

She thinks: Where do I begin?

Ryan leaves her office still feeling confused. Dr. Price realizes that she has much to learn about integrating faith and science to become an effective educator at a Christian University.

The concerns of these two fictional characters are real and recurring. A goal of this booklet is to help students and professors better understand the issues involved in the religion-science dialogue in general and the creation-evolution debate in particular.

---

[1] This vignette is adapted from Badger and Tenneson, "Does the Spirit Create through Evolutionary Processes? Pentecostals and Biological Evolution," in James K. A. Smith and Amos Yong, eds., *Science and the Spirit: A Pentecostal Engagement with the Sciences.* Indiana University Press, 2010, pp.92-116.

The Source of Conflict

We've heard the arguments between some creationists who act spiritually superior and some evolutionists who act intellectually superior. We've watched the nature programs on television with their assumption that all educated and intelligent viewers embrace the "evolution meta-narrative." Many of us were taught in Sunday school that all real Christians believe that God created the universe and all life a few thousands of years ago. This conflict causes many of us to feel enormous tension—if not outright turmoil—when we're asked to describe and defend a personal position on Origins.[2]

On the one hand, we pretty much accept most of the findings of science. Matter seems to behave in predictable patterns (e.g., Newton's laws of motion). The scientific practice of medicine has increased longevity and improved our quality of life. Almost every month technology provides us with better smart phones and tablet computers. We don't give this a second thought—instead we've come to expect it.

On the other hand, we have genuine, life-changing encounters with the living God. We know that he is real, and we try to allow God's Holy Spirit to guide our lives according to the Bible.

In the midst of this tension, some expert tells us that we can believe either the "biblical view" of a "recent" special creation or the scientifically popular view of an "ancient universe" and evolution. In order to accept any form of biological evolution, we are told, we must reject God's Word. But are these two the only possible choices?

The Contributions of Philosophy

Why Philosophy?

Some readers may be surprised that our discussion begins with philosophy instead of theology, biblical interpretation, the best translations of Hebrew words, or the conclusions of the natural sciences. Philosophy is that branch of knowledge that systematically examines basic concepts like reality, truth, existence, causality, and freedom. This second order discipline[3] helps us define technical terms, understand the methods of the natural sciences, recognize logical fallacies in arguments, and test truth claims. The natural sciences are a group of first-order disciplines since they study natural phenomena. So philosophy is foundational to our quest for truth and meaning—even in the natural sciences.

---

[2] In this work we capitalize *Origins* to indicate that we use this word to stand for the creation-evolution debate.

[3] Since philosophy often studies other disciplines (e.g.., philosophy of religion, philosophy of history, philosophy of art, etc.).

Beliefs, Knowledge, and Truth

How can we test statements about Origins to determine if they are true? Most people probably don't consciously think about why they believe what they believe, instead they accept what someone taught them.

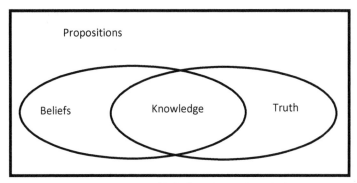

Figure 1: Relationship of belief, truth, and knowledge

The rectangle in Figure 1 above represents all statements (propositions) about Origins. The oval on the left represents a person's beliefs about Origins and the oval on the right represents true statements about Origins. The overlap represents knowledge.

So, knowledge is a belief that is true. Notice that some truth about Origins is not believed and some beliefs are not true. The first thing we need to do as we evaluate competing theories of Origins is to decide how we will evaluate various truth claims. What should our criteria be?

Do you think the physical realm exists independently of your mind? Look around you. If you are in a room, do you think that room still exists when you are far from it? If so, you are probably some type of a realist. (If not, you may be an idealist—but we hope that you function as a realist while driving a car or crossing a busy street!) Most of us almost certainly function as realists, but we may be a bit of both.

Figure 2 (on the next page) illustrates how a person's presuppositions affect an understanding of reality (part of epistemology) and affects our naturalistic or supernaturalistic view of Origins. These are represented along a continuum from absolute supernaturalism on the left to absolute naturalism on the right. Precisely where theists should be on each axis is debatable, but since they believe both the Special Revelation (e.g., the Bible) and the General Revelation (nature) describe reality, we should be in the middle somewhere.[4]

---

[4] This was adapted from Boehlke et.al., (2006) *Zygon* 41:2, 415-425.

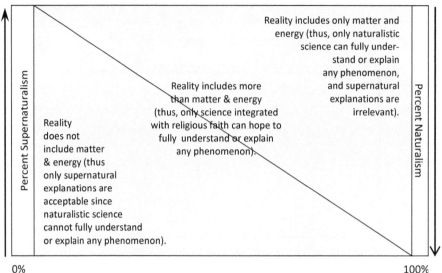

Reality includes only matter and energy (thus, only naturalistic science can fully understand or explain any phenomenon, and supernatural explanations are irrelevant).

Reality includes more than matter & energy (thus, only science integrated with religious faith can hope to fully understand or explain any phenomenon).

Reality does not include matter & energy (thus only supernatural explanations are acceptable since naturalistic science cannot fully understand or explain any phenomenon).

Percent Supernaturalism

Percent Naturalism

0%　　　　　　　　　　　　　　　　　　　　　　　　　100%

Figure 2: Naturalism vs. Supernaturalism

Whether they are realists or idealists, scientists, philosophers, and theologians may or may not embrace the Coherence Theory of Truth. This approach argues that a proposition is true if and only if it *coheres* (i.e., is consistent) with all other propositions in that "system." Thus, we embrace the Law of Noncontradiction, which claims that a statement cannot be true and false at the same time (if each of the terms in the statement are used with an identical meaning). The authors think that the coherence theory is a prerequisite condition, but not enough by itself, to determine the truth of a proposition.

The Correspondence Theory of Truth is used universally. This theory posits that a proposition is true if and only if it corresponds to the facts, or reality. Natural scientists use the approach, but so do people in many other disciplines, including biblical interpretation. The authors think that this test is also a prerequisite condition, but not enough by itself, to determine the truth of a proposition.

Only when a proposition passes both truth tests can a person be confident that he or she has arrived at "truth."

Norman Geisler summed this up nicely when he wrote, "Since all truth is God's truth, and since philosophy is a quest for truth, then philosophy will contribute to our understanding of God and his World."[5] We insist that these two truth tests should be foundational to answering questions of Origins.

---

[5] Geisler, Norman and Paul Feinberg. *Introduction to Philosophy: A Christian Perspective.* Grand Rapids: Baker Books, 1980, 1989, p.22.

Think of every statement that you believe is true about creation-evolution—every proposition—as occupying cells in a huge grid (like cells in a spreadsheet). Some cells are empty because of ignorance. Then you hear or read a statement about Origins that you've never heard before. As you try to fit it into your grid, you discover that it seems to contradict another statement that you have long embraced as true. What are your options? The easiest thing to do—and therefore what many people do—is just reject it as false. In order to embrace this new, seemingly non-coherent statement, you would have to do a lot of work reorganizing your entire grid, or at least part of it.

Your willingness to do this work depends on the strength of your precommitment to your grid versus the strength of your precommitment to discovering truth. Where does your allegiance lie? To maintaining your grid, or to discovering truth? We hope it is the latter.

Your theory of knowledge is part of your worldview and determines how you answer questions like these:

- What is knowledge?
- How do you know what you know?
- What are sources of knowledge?
- What are the limits of knowledge?
- How can you gain reliable knowledge?
- Do you gain reliable knowledge about different kinds of things using the same method, or by different methods?
- Should knowledge gained by different methods be integrated?
- Should you expect knowledge gained by different methods to be coherent?
- How can you evaluate and test "truth claims?"

Some people claim that the methods of the natural sciences are the only way to gain reliable knowledge about anything (this is scientism).[6] Others claim that the Bible is our best (or only) source of reliable answers to the questions of Origins. Still others accept the conclusions of the natural sciences for some things and believe the Bible in spiritual matters affecting their faith. Some people place unwarranted confidence in scientific methods and their practitioners while others place excessive confidence in the opinions of a charismatic Bible teacher or preacher.

But can scientific methods answer all of our questions? Or are scientific methods limited? The brief description of the scientific method provided in this

---

[6] Recognize that the premise of scientism (i.e., truth can be gained with confidence only via the scientific method) is a *philosophical* proposition, not a *scientific* statement. Further, just like "There are no absolute truths," it is a self-refuting statement (that is, it contradicts itself). Moreland and Craig remind us that self-refuting statements are necessarily false (348).

book suggests that it is limited to questions regarding the physical realm. But is the physical realm all that exists? And how do you know the answer to that question?

Does the Bible give us complete information about Origins? Do some people ask questions of the biblical texts that the original authors (human or divine) never intended to answer in that text?

What Do You Mean by *Evolution?*

Evolution is probably the most misunderstood term in the Origins debate. This technical term is used in a variety of ways in both the scientific and the popular literature, leading to confusion and pointless arguments. Some writers use evolution to describe changes in physical systems (e.g., galaxies, solar systems, and stars), but we limit our usage here to *biological* evolution (evolution in living systems). Biological evolution requires the passing on of genes and their associated physical traits from one generation to the next, and this cannot occur without RNA or DNA. Only living things naturally possess these molecules of inheritance, so only living things can evolve. Although some writers have identified as many as six meanings of *evolution* in biology textbooks, most people intend one of these three:[7]

- *Genetic change over time.* This may include minor changes or major changes and is usually measured by comparing gene frequencies in populations.

- *Common descent.* All living things have common ancestors. The more ancient the ancestor, the more different they may appear from organisms which live today. This is measured by physical and genetic similarities.

- *Materialism or naturalism.* The variety of life we see today and in the fossil record are the result of natural forces alone (God had nothing to do with it). The reader should note that this is a philosophical or religious approach, not empirical science, and the authors feel it is not an appropriate use of the term evolution.

Evolution is sometimes thought to include the idea of the origin of life. However, it doesn't. Evolutionary processes, like natural selection, can operate only if RNA or DNA is present. Evolution does not address how life came into being from non-life. Another common misconception about evolution is that individual organisms evolve, and then pass these changes on to their offspring. This idea of inheritance of acquired characteristics was popularized by the 18th and 19th century naturalist, Jean-Baptiste Lamarck, but it has since been soundly refuted by empirical evidence. Gene frequency changes are not measured in

---

[7] Meyer, S.C. and M. N. Keas, "The Meanings of Evolution" in *Darwinism, Design, and Public Education* eds. John A. Campbell and Stephen C. Meyer, (Rhetoric and Public Affairs Series), Michigan State University Press, 2003, 135-156.

individual organisms, instead, they are measured in *populations* over generations; thus, *populations*, not individuals, evolve.

Further, most biologists distinguish between *microevolution* and *macroevolution*. *Microevolution* describes changes in the genetic makeup of a population of organisms. The prefix "micro" indicates the changes are so small that the individuals that have "micro-evolved" can still interbreed with the original population. *Speciation* (formation of a new species) has not occurred. Virtually everyone accepts microevolution.

Macroevolution involves the same processes that cause microevolution. What differs is that the genetic makeup of the population has changed enough that the daughter population can no longer interbreed with the original population. *Speciation* has occurred. Many people who believe in limited change in the created species, or who find the neo-Darwinian explanations inadequate, reject macroevolution.[8]

Don't confuse the biological theory of macroevolution with the philosophy of evolutionism, which claims everything (not just life) is getting better (i.e., progressing). Don't assume that a person who accepts evolution necessarily embraces evolutionism.

We repeat this important thought: when discussing Origins, define technical terms—and ask others to do the same.

The Demarcation Problem

Some scientists think that a well-defined boundary exists between the sciences and the nonsciences, but this is not the case. Writers in various disciplines have long recognized the "demarcation problem," (i.e., what can we correctly call science?). The point is "What characteristics are found in science but are not found in nonscience?" Christian philosopher J. P. Moreland correctly concludes that there are no "generally accepted necessary and sufficient conditions for drawing a line of demarcation between science and nonscience."[9] Scientists and theologians must be willing to integrate ideas from other disciplines—especially as we consider creation-evolution. Since the boundary is not clear-cut, both scientists and theologians have contributions to make to the discussion on Origins.[10]

---

[8] Stern, David. "Perspective: Evolutionary Biology and the Problem of Variation," *Evolution,* 2000, 54, 1079.1091.

[9] Moreland, J. P. *Christianity and the Nature of Science.* Baker Books, 1989, p.42.

[10] People who would like to know more about the demarcation problem are encouraged to read one or more of the following: The first five or six pages of Stephen Meyer's "The Scientific Status of Intelligent Design: The Methodological Equivalence of Naturalistic and Non-Naturalistic Origins Theories" (available on the Internet at www.discovery .org/a/2834), J. P. Moreland's *Christianity and the Nature of Science: A Philosophical Investigation* (Baker Books, 1989), Larry Laudan's "The Demise of the Demarcation Problem," or Michael Shermer's *The Borderlands of Science: Where Sense Meets Nonsense.*(Oxford University Press, 2001).

Worldview and Origins

Because your beliefs about God and about how you can gain reliable knowledge are part of your *worldview*, your worldview plays a decisive role in determining which position on Origins you will embrace.

These worldview factors typically control a person's position on Origins:

1. Beliefs about God: Does he exist? What is his nature? Is he involved in the physical realm?

2. Beliefs about the Bible: Did God inspire the writing of Scripture? What does inspiration mean?

3. Beliefs about how a person gains reliable knowledge about Origins: Do you gain this knowledge by divine revelation, from the Bible, by scientific methods, or by the opinions of a prominent scientist or theologian?

4. Beliefs about the integration of knowledge: Can knowledge gained by different methods be integrated? If so, how can scientific knowledge be integrated with theological knowledge?

Those who conclude that God does not exist are not likely to try to gain knowledge about Origins from the Genesis creation account but will rely on scientific methods. Those who believe in God, on the other hand, are more likely to try to gain knowledge about Origins from the Genesis creation account. Some people try to integrate knowledge gained from both science and the Scriptures.

So what part should the Bible play in addressing questions of Origins? To help us answer this question, we will review some principles of interpreting the Bible, the methods of science, and patterns of integrating faith and science.

Philosophical Questions of Origins

Later we will consider several scientific questions and some theological questions, but here are some philosophical questions about science that Moreland and Craig raise: [11]

- What is science? Are there clear necessary and sufficient conditions that some intellectual activity must have for it to count as science? (Notice, this is the demarcation problem.)
- Is there such a thing as the scientific method?
- If the scientific method exists, what is it?
- Do scientific theories really explain things? If so, how?
- Can observational data really confirm a theory? If so, how?

Christians must be aware of the role of philosophy in helping us participate in the religion-science dialogue, but what role should the Bible and our interpretation of Scripture play in this conversation?

---

[11] Moreland, J.P. and William Lane Craig, *Philosophical Foundations for a Christian Worldview*, IVP, 2003, p. 308.

Divine Inspiration?

A foundational doctrine of the New Testament Church almost since its beginning has been the divine inspiration of the Scriptures. How do we know God inspired men to write the Bible? What does the phrase "God inspired the writing of Scripture" mean? We should avoid merely quoting Scripture to argue for divine inspiration of Scripture, since this is "circular reasoning."

Some portions of Scripture claim divine inspiration directly, for example: 1 Kings 12:22–24, 1 Chronicles 17:3-4, Jeremiah 35:13, Ezekiel 2:4, and Zechariah 7:9. These were introduced with phrases like these: "The word of God came to Shemaiah..."; "This is what the LORD says..."; and "The word of the LORD God came to Jeremiah...." Lindsell points out that something like this phrase can be found over 2,000 times in the Old Testament.[12] The account of Moses receiving the Ten Commandments from Yahweh is obviously a claim to divine inspiration.

The New Testament also supports inspiration of the Old Testament (e.g., Hebrews 1:1: "In the past God spoke to our ancestors through the prophets at many times and in various ways..." NIV). Both Paul and Peter wrote of the divine inspiration of Scripture:

> *But as for you, continue in what you have learned and have become convinced of, because you know those from whom you learned it, and how from infancy you have known the Holy Scriptures, which are able to make you wise for salvation through faith in Christ Jesus. All Scripture is God-breathed and is useful for teaching, rebuking, correcting and training in righteousness, so that the servant of God may be thoroughly equipped for every good work. (2 Tim. 3:14-17, NIV)*

> *Above all, you must understand that no prophecy of Scripture came about by the prophet's own interpretation of things. For prophecy never had its origin in the human will, but prophets, though human, spoke from God as they were carried along by the Holy Spirit. (2 Peter 1:20, NIV)*

Much other evidence for divine inspiration exists, including the fulfillment of scores of predictive prophecies (especially of the coming Messiah). Jesus affirmed that the Old Testament, and especially The Law, was true for all times (Matt. 5:8). He quoted or alluded to Old Testament passages repeatedly in his teachings, and thereby affirmed their authority.

Beyond these arguments (that some think should settle the matter), more than a century of archeological research in the Holy Land has confirmed the

---

[12] Lindsell, H. "Inspiration." Ed. by Merrill S. Tenney. *Zondervan Pictorial Encyclopedia of the Bible*, Vol. 3, p.289, Grand Rapids: Zondervan. 1976.

historicity of many portions of the Bible. The inspiration of Scripture has been accepted by the majority of Christian groups through the centuries. Finally, the inspiration of the Bible is supported by the testimony of countless hundreds of thousands of individual people over twenty centuries in virtually every place on earth who have experienced the truth of the Gospel.

Like so many other aspects of the science-faith interface, Christians hold a range of views on inspiration. Ask five different people what they mean when they say that they believe "the Bible was inspired by God," and we might get five different answers. Some would say that God dictated each and every word. Others believe that God inspired ideas, and the writer used his own words to communicate them. A few have even argued that the Bible contains God's Word, but is not wholly God's word, so readers must choose which parts are divinely inspired. Still others have compared inspiration to the descriptive definition intended by a musical composer who says that another person was her "inspiration" for a particular musical composition.

How would you describe your understanding of "the inspiration of Scripture"? Why do you hold your view? What convinces you to embrace your position?

Notice how a view of inspiration of the Bible is connected to a theory of knowledge. Why is divine inspiration of the Bible so important to believers? A person's convictions concerning the inspiration of Scripture will in large part control how he/she interprets and applies the Word of God. Divine inspiration is what gives Scripture its authority. Our conviction that the Bible is divinely inspired will also motivate us to read and study it so that we know what God tells us, and then to allow God's Spirit to transform our thinking and our behavior.

The Message of Genesis

The Old and New Testaments of the Bible both clearly and repeatedly identify God as the Creator of the physical realm and everything in it. Not only is the fact that God created everything revealed in Scripture, but his purposes in creating are also revealed.

What is God's message to us in the Genesis creation account? How can we hope to interpret it correctly? We must first answer two other questions (or groups of questions).

First, what is the literary form of the Genesis creation account? Scholars disagree over the best answer to this question. Some people identify the first part of Genesis as historical narrative. Others recognize that it has elements of ancient Hebrew poetry. Your identification of the literary form (genre) of the Genesis creation account will in part determine which theory of Origins you embrace.

This question raises other questions: Did God intend the Genesis creation account to be scientifically accurate (in terms of contemporary science)? Or was it written in terms of ancient non-scientific knowledge of the people of that time and place (accommodation)? Did the divine or human author of Genesis intend to reveal God's method in creating? If not, what was God trying to reveal in this passage? We must avoid asking questions of the text that the author never intended to address.

Second, how can we be confident that we have answered the questions in the previous two paragraphs accurately? Why do you answer those questions the way you do? In other words, how do you know what you know? What is your epistemological framework? Do we hold our opinions because this is what our parents or our church tradition taught us? Or does the evidence push us to our conclusions?

Let's summarize the major points of the first few chapters of Genesis.

1. The universe and everything in it had a beginning.

2. Human history had a beginning and will have an end.

3. There is only one God, and He is Yahweh.

4. God is personally and intimately involved in His creation.

5. God considered the creation good.

6. God created everything—including life—in the physical universe.

7. God brought everything into existence for His own purposes.

8. Humans (and only humans) are created in God's image.

9. God created humans to live in loving relationship with him and with each other.

10. The first humans disobeyed God (sin), destroying our relationship with God.

11. God punished humans for disbelieving and disobeying Him.

12. The rest of Genesis—indeed, the rest of the Bible—reveals God's great desire for fellowship with humans to be restored.

Notice that this list does not include when God created (other than "in the beginning") or how God created—just that he did, why he did, and the consequences of his creation of humans. Scholars raise many other questions concerning the meaning of the Genesis creation account, but space does not permit us to address all of them.

While it is true that the integrative pattern (Two Worlds, Conflict, Concordism, etc.) you employ will greatly affect which Origins position (YEC, OEC, EC)[13] you accept, your answers to questions such as those below will also help determine how you interpret the first part of Genesis. So, consider how you answer these questions, and—just as important—why you answer these questions the way you do:[14]

1. What is the literary form of the Genesis creation account? Is it historical

---

[13] Young Earth Creationists, Old Creationists, Evolutionary Creationists.

[14] Appendix 2 addresses these concepts in much more depth.

narrative? Is it poetical? Is it accurate in terms of modern science?

2. Does a treatment of the Genesis creation account as scientifically accurate historical narrative pose any problems? If so, can these problems be solved?

3. Is accepting the Genesis creation account as scientifically accurate historical narrative crucial to genuine New Testament faith?

4. What is the range of meaning of the Hebrew word *yom* (translated into English as *day*)? Must this be understood as a 24-hour period?

5. Finally, are you simply discovering the meaning in the Bible? Or are you reading meanings into the text that are not there?

Everyone finds it difficult to answer the questions above honestly, completely, and accurately.

What is our point here? We must first wrestle with the questions raised above—and other questions too—before we can arrive at a tentative conclusion on Origins.

Theological Questions of Origins

People who place a high value on Scripture might argue that this is the only source of reliable knowledge regarding Origins. But we should not forget Romans 1:18-20, in which the Apostle Paul, under the inspiration of the Holy Spirit, told his readers that God's power and nature are clearly seen from what He has made. Let's offer a few theological questions.

- Should we read the Bible as a divine document, a human document, or both?
- Did a Supreme Being cause the physical realm to come into existence?
- If so, is the God of the Bible that Being? In not, who/what was?
- Does the physical realm have a purpose?
- If so, do humans have a purpose? If so, what is that purpose?
- Is the physical realm, good, bad, or neither?
- What is the literary form of the Genesis creation account and how should we interpret it?

The Contributions of the Natural Sciences

Scientific Methods

Science is a group of methods used to answer questions and solve problems regarding natural phenomena. The two central features of scientific methods are observation and experimentation. Once a question or problem has been identified, the scientist gathers as much information as he/she can about the question or problem via the five physical senses (or instrumental extensions of these senses). Then a tentative explanation (hypothesis) is proposed, and experiments are designed and constructed to test the hypothesis. A process of refining and re-testing the hypothesis leads the scientist to answers/solutions.

Typically other scientists will repeat the experiments and confirm the observations and conclusions. Table 1 lists some of the advantages and disadvantages of the scientific method.

Advantages	Disadvantages
Essentially objective	Practitioners are subjective[15]
Empirical	Limited to natural phenomena
Testable	Unavoidable uncertainty
Systematic	Cannot answer questions of aesthetics
Repeatable	Cannot answer questions of ethics

Table 1: Characteristics and limitations of science

We intentionally limit this booklet to the "natural sciences": the biological sciences, physics, and chemistry. This is not intended to discredit the "behavioral sciences" or the "social sciences." We're just limiting ourselves to what we know.

Not everyone agrees there is such a thing as "The Scientific Method." Instead, they argue, there are scientific methods (plural).[16] This is not a new idea. As early as 1966 Ian Barbour wrote,

> At the outset it should be stated that there is no "scientific method," no formula with five easy steps guaranteed to lead to discoveries. There are many methods, used at different stages of inquiry, in widely different circumstances.[17]

Scientific methods have been used to gain reliable, useful answers to numerous questions and solutions to various problems—all related to natural phenomena. For example, we used it to learn that a liquid absorbs heat as it evaporates and then applied that knowledge to build refrigerators and air conditioners. We used it to learn what causes many diseases and then applied that knowledge to prevent or cure those illnesses.

---

[15] Richard Sternberg, non-Christian evolutionary biologist, was disciplined by the Smithsonian Institution for accepting an Intelligent Design proponent's (Stephen Meyer) paper for publication in the journal he edited.

[16] Moreland and Craig agree that "there is no such thing as *the* scientific method, but rather there is a cluster of practices and issues that are used in a variety of contexts and can be loosely called scientific methodologies" (310). They go on to propose an eclectic model and describe seven characteristics of this model (313-324).

[17] Barbour, Ian G. *Issues in Science and Religion.* Prentice-Hall, 1966.

But do these methods allow us to answer the questions of what happened thousands or millions of years ago—things that apparently happened just once in history? Scientists may propose hypotheses about Origins, but they usually cannot design experiments that will reconstruct the historical setting needed to test their hypotheses.

For this reason, some scholars (like Stephen Meyer) distinguish between observable (empirical) experimental science and historical science. JP Moreland and William Lane Craig describe them like this:

> Empirical science...focuses on how the natural world operates in a repeatable and regular way. Historical science...focuses on single, past events (e.g., the death of dinosaurs, the origin of first life) and attempts to explain how things came to be or why some event happened.[18]

In other words, can empirical science provide answers to questions about Origins in the same ways that it has answered other questions? We ask this question because we cannot use our hypotheses about Origins to construct experiments to test them in the same way that we test other hypotheses. Consequently, some scholars think much of the Origins debate that passes as "science" is more correctly labeled "philosophy." This is not to say that it is wrong, just to recognize what it is and is not.

While scientific methods lend themselves to objectivity, the people who use them are typically as subjective as other people. In other words, scientists can be and often are as biased as any other group of people.

If a person believes the methods of science are able to answer all questions and solve all problems, that person is likely to embrace whatever theory of Origins is popular among scientists at that time.

How a scientist practices science is largely determined by his or her philosophy of science (*e.g.*, embracing naturalism).[19] Scientists also approach their investigations with presuppositions and assumptions.[20] Virtually everyone

---

[18] Moreland & Craig, *Philosophical Foundations for a Christian Worldview.* IVP, 2003, p. 320. They repeat this on page 363: "Recall that empirical science is a non-historical, empirical approach to the world that focuses on repeatable, regularly recurring events or patterns in nature (*e.g.*, the relationship between pressure, temperature, and volume in a gas). By contrast, historical science...focuses on past singularities that are not repeatable (*e.g.*, the origin of the universe, first life, various kinds of life)."

[19] For a more comprehensive list of philosophical presuppositions of science, see Moreland and Craig, 348.

[20] Moreland and Craig list five core tenets of scientific realism and summarize it like this: "Science involves some form of the correspondence theory of truth: A theory is true if and only if what it says about the world is in fact the way the world is" (328). Later they go on to say that "the defense or rebuttal of scientific realism illustrates the fact that the philosophy of science is presuppositional to science itself. That is, the question of how we should understand the existence claims of a given scientific theory will be answered, in part, by one's attitude toward scientific realism, and one's attitude about this will, in turn, be justified largely in philosophical terms" (Moreland and Craig, 332).

seeking knowledge assumes self-existence and the existence of other people and things—and acts as if communication is possible. Scientists also use these presuppositions:

1. Nature is measurable, understandable, knowable, orderly, and regular.
2. Natural phenomena are reproducible and can be described mathematically.
3. Natural laws do not change with time (uniformitarianism).

Of these presuppositions, the only one that is often challenged in the Origins debate is uniformitarianism.

Introduced by geologist Charles Lyell in the mid-1800s, the Principle of Uniformitarianism posits that the physical processes that occurred in the past are still in action today and are occurring at the same rates. This idea directly opposes the Principle of Catastrophism championed in the early 1800s by paleontologist Georges Cuvier. Historical and predictive science both depend on the uniformitarianism assumption. Otherwise the conclusions of historical and predictive science are suspect.

Practitioners of empirical science often collect and graph data and then extend the graph beyond the known data (see Figure 3). We can call the extension into the future "predictive science" and extension into the past "historical science" (dashed lines on the graph). But we cannot have the same level of confidence in the extensions as we do in the "empirical science" (solid line on the graph).[21]

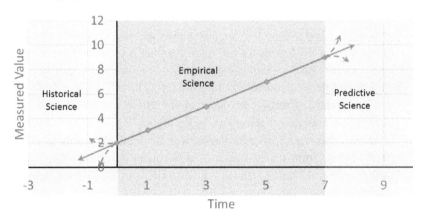

Figure 3: Comparison of historical, empirical, & predictive science

Origins: Five Camps

Contemporary attempts to answer the questions of Origins can be arranged into five general viewpoints. Below we will use the popular names of each group—despite objections by some as to what they want to be called.

---

[21] Technically, we do not know the position of the line between the data points in the middle section; we know only the five data points.

People who belong to the first three camps listed below (YEC, OEC, EC) believe in the God of the Bible and agree that the Bible is God's Word (although they disagree about how the creation accounts in the Bible should be understood). Christians typically belong to one of the first three groups.

1. Young Earth Creationists (YEC) prefer to call their position "Scientific Creation." YEC typically interpret the biblical creation accounts as scientifically accurate historical narrative. Thus, they claim that both the Bible and scientific evidences support these conclusions: (1) God suddenly made the physical realm and life, (2) out of nothing, (3) in six consecutive 24-hour periods, (4) about 6,000-15,000 years ago. (5) All theories of macroevolution are rejected, (6) as is a universe that is billions of years old. Ken Ham, Duane Gish, and Henry Morris are some of the most widely known adherents of YEC.

2. Old Earth Creationists (OEC) accept the scientific evidences for a universe that is billions of years old, but they argue that God created everything— including life—by a series of creative acts that took place over a long period of time. This position is also known as "Progressive Creation." Adherents often disagree on when each of these creative acts occurred. OEC generally reject macroevolution but believe that God directly created life pretty much as it exists today. Creation accounts in the Bible are interpreted as historical narrative but not necessarily as a scientific explanation of how God created. Hugh Ross is probably the most widely known contemporary proponent of OEC.

3. Evolutionary Creationists (EC) are also known as theistic evolutionists. They accept the scientific evidence for a universe that is billions of years old and embrace contemporary biological theories of evolution, but they stress that God guided the evolution of existing life forms from the original life forms that He created. Creation accounts in the Bible are not thought to be historical narrative or scientifically accurate. EC generally attempt to harmonize theories of macroevolution with the biblical account of Origins. Many EC question the existence of a historical Adam and Eve. Francis Collins, Kenneth Miller, Howard J. van Till, and Denis Lamoureux are advocates of EC.

4. The fourth group, the Deistic Evolutionists (DE), claims that God is no longer involved in the physical realm. They also usually maintain that the physical realm is a superior and more trustworthy revelation of God than the Bible (which is usually rejected as neither inspired nor authoritative). DE argue that if God created the physical realm, He left it to evolve on its own. Charles Darwin represented this position.

5. Since Atheistic Evolutionists (AE) deny the existence of God, they propose that life arose from non-life via natural causes. They also posit that one kind of life changed into other kinds of life by natural processes. AE do not consider the Bible to be God's Word. People who are not necessarily

confirmed atheists, but who attempt to answer the questions of Origins without invoking God, could also be included in this camp. Some people call this Ateleological (purposeless) Evolution. Richard Dawkins is an outspoken, well-known AE.

Camp	God...	The Bible...	Reliable knowledge....
AE	Does not exist	Is a collection of ancient myths of value only as literature	About Origins is gained only via the scientific methods
DE	Exists, but is not involved in His creation	Is inferior to the physical realm in gaining knowledge about God	About Origins is gained only via scientific methods
EC	Is the Creator-Redeemer described in the Bible	Creation account is not historical narrative; thus God did not intend it to convey a scientific description of Origins and how and when He accomplished His creation	About Origins is gained primarily via science, but the Scriptures may inform our theory of Origins
OEC	Is the Creator-Redeemer described in the Bible	Creation account may be historical narrative; thus God may not have intended it to convey a scientific description of Origins and how and when He accomplished His creation	About Origins is gained both from the Scriptures and science; thus, our theory of Origins should integrate findings of both
YEC	Is the Creator-Redeemer described in the Bible	Creation account is historical narrative; thus God intended it to convey a scientific description of Origins and how and when He accomplished His creation	About Origins is gained first from the Scriptures and then from scientific methods

Table 2: How presuppositions affect camp affiliation

Table 2 is a summary of how your viewpoints about God, the Bible, and epistemology affect your conclusions about Origins.

While some people (*e.g.*, Buddhists and Hindus) may not fall into one of these five groups, this is a general description of the vast majority of Westerners today.[22] Over 1,500Pentecostal students, educators, and pastors in recent surveys developed and administered by the authors lead to the findings in Table 3.

Camp	Percentage
Young Earth Creation	20-40
Old Earth Creation	20-40
Theistic Evolution	15-20
Undecided and Blank	25

Table 3: Origins positions of Pentecostals

Pentecostals do not uniformly embrace a single position on Origins.

The "Gap Theory" posits a large time gap between the first two verses in Genesis and is illustrated in Figure 4 below. The first verse of Genesis 1 supposedly describes the original creation followed by destruction and a long time period; the rest of the chapter describes the recent creation account. Few scholars today embrace the Gap Theory.[23]

The conclusion a person reaches regarding creation-evolution often depends on two things: the confidence that person has in the methods of science to answer the questions of Origins and the confidence he or she has in a particular interpretation of the Genesis creation account. Figure 4 illustrates this. The blurred edges of each camp are meant to indicate the fact that no camp is monolithic, and there is some overlap between camps.

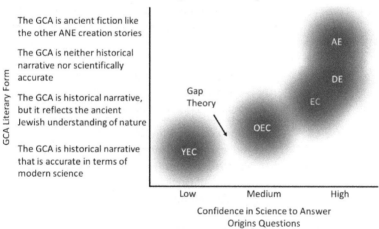

Figure 4: Confidence in Science vs Confidence in View of GCA[24]

---

[22] A few ancient Near Eastern myths include creation stories (*e.g.*, "The Gilgamesh Epic," "Enuma Elish," and "Enki and Ninhursag"). Consult almost any commentary on Genesis or a Bible encyclopedia for more information.

[23] The Gap Theory was popularized by inclusion in some study Bibles in the 20th century, but it is not favored by conservative Old Testament scholars today.

[24] Appendix 1 has a tool to help you map your own position.

Proposed Evidences for Macroevolution

Below are a few of the typical arguments and evidences that have convinced some people to embrace contemporary macroevolutionary theory.

1. The Age of Creation. The majority of scientists think that the scientific evidence points to a physical realm that is billions of years old. Since most scientists haven't found the criticisms of radiometric dating convincing, they generally conclude the earth and other parts of creation are ancient. While this does not prove macroevolution, it is prerequisite. If the earth were known to be only thousands of years old, theories of macroevolution would be rejected.[25]

2. Natural and Artificial Selection. Natural selection posits that individuals in a population possess a variety of genetically based characteristics. Members of a population can have much variation in certain traits. Depending on the organism's habitat, some of these characteristics favor survival and reproductive success more than others. Consequently, individuals that possess the favorable traits produce more offspring than those that lack them. After several generations, this favorable trait becomes more common in the population, and the less favorable trait becomes rarer. In the short term, this can lead to microevolution (genetic and physical changes that don't result in speciation), and over the long term, macroevolution (speciation).

The findings of many empirical studies fit the theory of natural selection. They include studies of the development of antibiotic-resistant strains of bacteria, the size of guppies in relation to the size of predators, and the correlation of Galapagos Finch beak thickness with seed toughness (due to the amount of rainfall).

Natural selection is similar to artificial selection, in which humans selectively breed animals or plants to produce offspring with the desired traits.

---

[25] We are not suggesting that the only tenable viewpoints on Origins depend on an old earth. However, the *scientific* evidence is overwhelming in support of an ancient universe and earth. In 1997, the Institute for Creation Research and the Creation Research Society (YEC advocates) funded a research program called RATE (Radioisotopes and the Age of The Earth). Volume I of the final report was published in 2000 and volume II in 2005. The report concludes that:

1) there is very strong evidence of more than 500 million years of radioactive decay;

2) a young earth is evidenced by Biblical interpretation and a few scientific studies;

3) decay rates must have been accelerated by a factor of approximately one billion during days 1-3 of creation and the flood;

4) although not explainable now, the removal of heat and other forms of radiation will be explained in the future; and

5) as a result the RATE project strongly supports the reliability of the Bible.

The last four points depend on the falsity of uniformitarianism, which is a minority position among scientists—both theists and non-theists.

See Vardiman, L. *Assessing the RATE Project*. Essay Review in Perspectives on Science and Christian Faith, 59(2), June 2007, (143-146).

The effect of artificial selection has been enormous. Consider the many breeds of dogs, horses, and pigeons. Many people don't know that cabbage, Brussels sprouts, and broccoli are all derived from the mustard plant. In a relatively short period of time, humans have drastically altered the genetically controlled features of these domesticated plants and animals. Many scientists think that natural selection could have even greater effects over long periods of time.[26]

3. Biogeography. The study of the geographic distribution of life forms (both living and fossils) presents a variety of interesting relationships. One example is the matching Triassic reptile fossils in West Africa and Brazil (there is evidence these continents were once joined). Another example is the concentration of marsupials in Australia (but not on the other continents). These fossil evidences and the continental drift theory of geology are consistent with macroevolutionary theory.

4. The Fossil Record. The fossil record is rich and diverse. Many people (including some theists) find the catastrophic flood explanation insufficient to explain the distribution and abundance of discovered fossils. Although not complete, most scientists believe the fossil record is better explained by macroevolution (uniformitarianism) than by catastrophism.

Fossils include any preserved remains (including burrows, feces, footprints) of formerly living things. Radiometric dating indicates these fossils range in age from thousands to billions of years old. The fossil record is incomplete because they were formed relatively rarely—most dead plants and animals were consumed or decomposed. Thus the fossil record represents only a tiny fraction of the variety of life that existed.

Our interpretations of the fossil record would improve greatly if fossils contained DNA that could be analyzed for genetic similarities. From these data, stronger inferences could be made about ancestral relationships. Unfortunately, scientists have been unable to isolate DNA from fossils. Thus, paleontologists must depend on the methods of historical science to interpret the fossil record.

Paleontologists report on numerous transitional fossils in two groups of vertebrates: the reptile/bird transition and the amphibious/aquatic transition in whales. Recent discoveries of feather-bearing reptile fossils have caused a stir. The older reptilian fossils (based on radiometric dating) bear non-flight feathers, whereas flight feathers are found only in the more recent ones. Aside from feathers, these creatures appear in all other ways to be reptilian. Bird fossils, with their lack of reptilian features, do not appear until the most recent geologic strata. Consider another example: the most ancient whale fossils possess hind limbs, whereas the more recent (and living) whales lack these structures.[27]

---

[26] Some writers argue that artificial selection is not a good analogue to natural selection because artificial selection is teleological (goal-oriented), whereas natural selection is ateleological (not goal-oriented).

[27] In recent years, *The National Geographic Magazine* and other magazines have published several articles about these fossils and the developing family tree for

5. Vestigial Structures. Vestigial structures are anatomical features that have no known or greatly reduced function compared to apparent ancestors. These features are considered to confer no selective advantage to their owners and are thought to be a remnant of an ancestral use. Snakes are used as an example of this. Taking into account DNA similarities and the fossil record, snakes are thought to have evolved from lizards. The "primitive" snakes (boas, pythons) possess small pelvic bone structures embedded in their muscle walls—with no known function. The other groups of snakes lack these structures.

6. Biochemistry. Scientists have compared the similarities and differences in the structure of a variety of biochemicals in different species. Cytochrome c, a protein necessary for cellular respiration, is found in all life that uses oxygen. The chemical structure of cytrochrome c is very similar among all life forms, showing only a few amino acid differences throughout the complete range of living things. This is suggested as evidence of a common ancestor for all life.[28]

7. Logical & Reasonable. Generally, macroevolution fits two common "Truth Tests." It generally "hangs together," and thus fits the Coherence Theory of Truth. And it generally seems to correspond to what little empirical evidence we have and thus fits the Correspondence Theory of Truth (which in turn depends on the existence of a "theory-independent" world).

In sum, most (but not all) biologists today use macroevolution as the unifying theory of biology because they think the evidences and arguments cited above (along with others) sufficiently support it.

Gradual or Sudden?

Charles Darwin, who, along with Alfred Russell Wallace, developed the theory of natural selection, believed that evolution occurred gradually over time. Some modern evolutionary biologists, like the late Stephen Jay Gould and Niles Eldridge, have theorized that macroevolution happened in "bursts" of rapid change with long periods of little or no change between. This theory, punctuated equilibrium, was introduced in 1972 and has gained wide acceptance among contemporary biologists and paleontologists. Interestingly, it explains the same sudden appearance of new kinds of life in the fossil record that OEC posits.

---

feathered reptiles. Interestingly, in 2000, they also published a retraction of a report on "Archaeoraptor," a fossil that was determined to be fake. But numerous other feathered reptile fossils support the theory of an evolutionary connection between reptiles and birds.

[28] On the other hand, other biochemicals differ greatly between groups of organisms. One example is the amino acid sequence in the human hemoglobin polypeptide. Animals that are theorized to be closely related to humans due to recent common ancestry (e.g., monkeys) share about 95% of the amino acid sequence with humans. Animals that are thought to be more distantly related to humans (e.g., frogs) share only about 54% of amino acid sequence in the same molecule. Some molecules don't seem to fit well into the taxonomic schemes, and much debate exists among taxonomists about how to handle these anomalies.

Intelligent Design

The theory of Intelligent Design (ID), advocated by William Paley in the early 1800s, has gained momentum in recent years among Christians. The theory is summarized thus: "...intelligent causes are necessary to explain the complex, information-rich structures of biology and...these causes are empirically detectable."[29]

Three of the best known modern proponents of ID are mathematician and philosopher William Dembski, biochemist Michael Behe, and philosopher Stephen Meyer. They offer two main arguments to support ID.

Specified complexity (Dembski and Meyer) is based on the claim that living things are complex in ways that undirected random processes could never produce. Statistical analyses of DNA support this argument. They argue that chance alone can produce complex unspecified information and noncomplex specified information, but it cannot produce complex specified information. By a process of elimination, complex specified information is best explained by ID.

Behe presents irreducible complexity as another line of evidence. A single living system is composed of several (often many) interacting parts. Each one contributes to the basic function of the system. Removal of any one of the components causes the system to cease functioning. Furthermore, no functional intermediates that lack some of the parts are known. Behe illustrates this with the biochemistry of blood clotting and the structure and function of bacterial flagella (among others).

Charles Darwin recognized this potential risk to his theory of natural selection: "If it could be demonstrated that any complex organ existed which could not possibly have been formed by numerous, successive, slight modifications, my theory would absolutely break down."[30] ID proponents often use this quote to challenge Darwinism.

Since materialistic biologists have failed to provide satisfactory natural explanations for the origin and development of these complex biological systems, ID is presented as a better explanation than naturalistic evolution.

ID is consistent with the idea of a "finely tuned universe."[31] Scientists have long recognized that the universe is special—it is finely tuned to support life. Consider this incomplete list of seemingly arbitrary and unrelated physical constants:

- Nuclear strong force

---

[29] William Paley, *Natural Theology; or, Evidences of the Existence and Attributes of the Deity*, 12th ed. London: J. Faulder, 1809, (1).

[30] Darwin, Charles. *The Origin of Species By Means of Natural Selection Or The Preservation of Favored Races in the Struggle for Life*. Modern Library, 1998, (232).

[31] Barr, Stephen M. *Modern Physics and Ancient Faith*. Notre Dame: Notre Dame Press, 2003; and Whorton, Mark and Hill Roberts. *Holman QuickSource Guide to Understanding Creation*. B&H Publishing, 2008.

- Nuclear weak force
- Electromagnetic coupling constant
- Ratio of electron to proton mass
- Entropy level of the universe
- Force of gravity
- Cosmological constant

These physical constants have precisely the values essential for a universe that can support life as we know it. Small changes in these constants would correspond to a very different universe without stars and solar systems—one in which life as we know it could not exist.

Many theists see God as the designer behind the finely tuned universe. On the other hand, non-theists tend to argue for explanations involving chance or the existence of many universes (multiverse theory).

Intelligent Design theories have not dramatically affected which camp creationists embrace (YEC, OEC, EC), but they are consistent with the notion of a Creator (designer).[32] Also, they have raised the awareness of philosophical arguments in the Origins debate (e.g., the movie "Expelled" by Ben Stein, which exposed the strong naturalistic bias of the scientific community).

ID is defended as a scientific approach (and not simply old fashioned creationism masquerading as science) because it produces empirically testable hypotheses. ID researchers have made four major predictions:[33]

1. "Natural structures will be found that contain many parts arranged in intricate patterns that perform a specific function..."

2. "Forms containing large amounts of novel information will appear in the fossil record suddenly and without similar precursors."

3. "Convergences will occur routinely. That is, genes and other functional parts will be re-used in different and unrelated organisms."

4. "Much 'junk DNA' will turn out to perform valuable functions."

Critics of ID raise several objections. The first is that ID isn't really science because it invokes supernatural factors as part of a conclusion. Since most scientists embrace a naturalistic worldview that rejects the consideration of any supernatural agency, they reject the notion that science should ever include theistic elements.[34] Some creationists view it as being too watered down, since it

---

[32] Luskin, C. *The Positive Case for Design.* Discovery Institute Fact Sheet, available at http://www.discovery.org/scripts/viewDB/filesDB-download.php?command=download&id=546 (accessed 6/2007).

[33] Moreland and Craig agree: "However, when applied to the issue of evolution...the ID movement does not map neatly onto the three views" (356).

[34] "The statements of science must invoke only natural things and processes" (National Academy of Sciences. *Teaching About Evolution and the Nature of Science,* The Academy Press, 1998 (42).) "Even if all the data point to an intelligent designer, such an hypothesis is excluded from science because it is not naturalistic" (Scott C. Todd,

doesn't explicitly name the designer as the God of the Bible, while others oppose it because some ID proponents accept macroevolution.

Among creationists, the most serious objection is that ID is a "God of the gaps" approach, limiting itself to explaining only what science cannot. As scientific data expand, the gaps are replaced with scientific theories, and divine explanations are discarded. The confidence Christians have in the Bible is undermined as we have less and less need to invoke God as the causative agent.

A person's worldview probably pre-determines how he or she feels about ID. Theists tend to overlook the theory's weaknesses, atheists tend to overlook the theory's strengths, and creationists are split—some favor it while others oppose it.

Scientific Questions of Origins

Through the years, people have asked many various questions—and proposed many various answers—regarding Origins. The debate involves much more than answering the question "Which actually happened—evolution or creation?" Consider the following *scientific* questions that are part of this ultimate riddle:

- Did the physical universe have a beginning? Or did it always exist?
- If it began, how and when did the physical realm come into existence?
- How and when did our solar system come into existence?
- When and how did life come into existence?
- How and when did the varieties of life arise?
- When and how did human life come into existence?
- Did humans and other life forms originate the same way?
- Is there a purpose for our existence?

Where do your answers to the above questions fit in the Figure 1? Are your answers beliefs or knowledge? How certain are you of your answers?

Integration

Patterns of Integration

Why should we attempt to integrate scientific knowledge with our faith? Some reply, "All truth is God's truth," and Christians are searching for truth (reality) not only about this world, but about our ultimate, spiritual world with God. Others might cite Romans 1:18-20 as support for the position that God is revealed not only in the Scriptures, but also in creation, the physical universe.

The wrath of God is being revealed from heaven against all the godlessness and wickedness of people, who suppress the truth by their wickedness, since what may be known about God is plain to them,

Department of Biology, Kansas State University. "A View from Kansas on that Evolution Debate." *Nature*, Vol. 12, Sept. 30, 1999, (423).

because God has made it plain to them. For since the creation of the world God's invisible qualities—his eternal power and divine nature—have been clearly seen, being understood from what has been made, so that people are without excuse. (NIV)

What does nature reveal about God? His power and godly (divine) nature. We don't suggest that God's offer of forgiveness and all of his plans for humans is revealed in the physical universe. But we doubt most of us reflect on and consider how nature can inform our faith in God. Figure 5 below reminds us that our understanding of God's word and our understandings of nature both are based on (fallible) human interpretation.

How do people integrate their understanding of science with their Christian faith? What credence do people place on their understanding of the General Revelation (Nature) versus their understanding of the Special Revelation (the Bible)? Many people overlook the fact that both science and biblical theology depend on *human interpretation*. In large part, this is why neither discipline is infallible. Figure 5 below is an attempt to illustrate this.

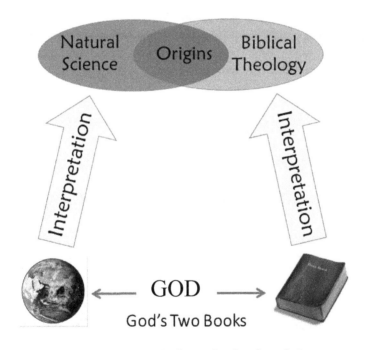

Figure 5: God's two books of revelation

Below are five general patterns of integration of knowledge gained via the natural sciences and knowledge gained via biblical studies.[35]

No Common Ground: "Science and theology tell us different kinds of things about different things."[36] Conflict is impossible by definition because natural science and biblical theology have no common ground. Each discipline should address only those issues in its own domain. This pattern is called "Compartmentalism," NOMA (Non-Overlapping Magisteria), or The Two Worlds View. The American Association for the Advancement of Science has adopted this position, which is illustrated below.

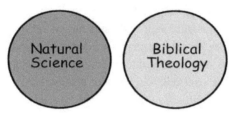

Figure 6: No common ground

Scientists Know Best: "Science and theology tell us the same kinds of things about the same things."[37] When they conflict, both cannot be right. In any conflict, science is always right. Contemporary theology must be revised to be consistent with the developments and discoveries of contemporary science. The figure below illustrates this position.

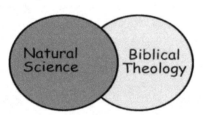

Figure 7: Scientists know best

Theologians Know Best: "Science and theology tell us the same kinds of things about the same things."[38] When they conflict, both cannot be right. In any conflict, theology is always right. The scientific description of the world provides us with such overwhelming evidence of the truth of biblical theology that our only logical choice is to believe the Bible is true. The figure below illustrates this position.

---

[35] For a somewhat different presentation of models of integration, see Moreland and Craig's *Philosophical Foundations for a Christian Worldview*, (350f).

[36] Bube, Putting It All Together, p. 95.

[36] Ibid., p.55 and 129.

[38] Ibid., p. 75 and 102.

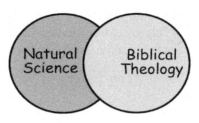

Figure 8: Theologians know best

Both Are Right: "Science and theology tell us different kinds of things about the same things."[39] When true to its capabilities and limitations, each discipline provides valid insights into the nature of reality, but from different perspectives. An adequate and coherent view of reality can be obtained only if people (and their professional communities) integrate these two disciplines. This is often called "Complementarism" and is illustrated below.

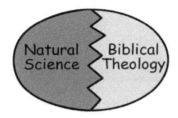

Figure 9: Both are right

Both Are Wrong: "Science and theology should tell us the same kinds of things about the same things." [40] The inability of contemporary biblical theology and natural science to agree is due to human imperfection in both disciplines. Both science and theology need to find new approaches to achieve an integrated understanding of reality. This is often called "Concordism" and is illustrated below.

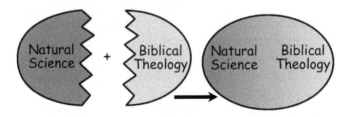

Figure 10: Neither is correct by itself

---

[39] Ibid., p.167.

[40] Ibid., p.143.

Not all of these patterns are useful for Christians. Identifying your own pattern of integration can help you start to answer the questions of Origins. We think Complementarism and Concordism are better choices for Christians.[41]

Conclusions

Whom Should I Ask?

Philosophy is the appropriate discipline to address some questions (e.g., what is the definition of science?); the natural sciences are better suited to answering some questions (e.g., what is the density of methylene chloride at standard temperature and pressure?); and biblical theology is the appropriate discipline to answer some questions (e.g., who was Jesus of Nazareth?). But some questions are best answered by interaction between specialists in two or more disciplines. For example, biologists, philosophers, and theologians should collaborate to find answers to questions involving human life. This is just one of the reasons why the religion-science dialogue is important—and why we think Christians should be actively involved.

Its Value

What is the value in the life of a believer to know that God is the Creator? Let us suggest a few reasons. First, we want you to believe it because it is true. Jesus taught that "the truth will set you free" (John 8:32, NIV). If the truth sets people free, what effect will a falsehood have? Falsehoods can enslave us.

While we posit that the Bible does not reveal *how* or *when* God created, without question it does reveal *who* and *why*. God created humans to have and enjoy a unique relationship with him. (But our lack of belief and disobedience (i.e., sin) destroyed that relationship.)

Second, recognizing God as Creator helps us to see ourselves as *creatures* (created beings). The Bible paints many pictures of the relationship God has and/or will have with us (e.g., Master/servant, Shepherd/sheep, Savior/saved, etc.). Prior to all of these is the relationship of Creator/creature. This should remind us of God's sovereignty over all of his creation, including us humans.

Third, the Bible presents only humans as being created in the image of God. While this is one of the most difficult truths to understand, it does help us to appreciate why God loved us enough to send a Savior to redeem us.

Fourth, several portions of Scripture teach that God's plan of salvation includes his Holy Spirit transforming us into holy people bearing and exhibiting the fruit of his Spirit (Gal 5:22) . These traits are not gained by our ability to "turn over a new leaf" but by yielding to and working with the Creator to "create in me a clean heart" (Psalm 51:10). Knowing that God is the one who created

---

[41] After reading more on these patterns, one of the authors (Badger) has been weakening on embracing Concordism as a good model of integration, favoring Complementarism instead.

the physical realm gives us confidence that he is able to transform us into Christlikeness.

Our Intent

We wrote this book to try to explain the main issues involved in understanding the principal positions people embrace concerning creation and evolution. Although we have endeavored to avoid promoting any one of the three theistic models of Origins that conservative Christians embrace, we realize that we probably have not completely succeeded.

Beyond this, we hope we have encouraged fellow believers to consider the reasons why they hold the opinions on Origins that they do. We think that this examination will result in a more solid faith in the Savior and improve relationships among Christians who disagree on Origins. Finally, we hope that this book will help equip believers to discuss Origins with scientifically literate non-Christians who are seeking the truth.

Should We Be Dogmatic?

How strongly should Christians hold their views on Origins? We consider these doctrines non-negotiable: God is the Creator of all; God created only humans in His image; and the Bible is the only inspired Word of God.

On the other hand, some of the questions of Origins cannot be answered with a high degree of certainty by either natural scientists or Bible-believing theologians. Neither of these groups has presented conclusive proof of precisely how or when God did his creation work.

Finally, Christians should realize that while it is crucial that we recognize God as the Creator, it is not crucial that we all reach a firm conclusion on the details of when and how God created. Admitting ignorance here may be wisdom.

How Can You Use This Information?

Positions on Origins are like sunglasses. Once you put them on, they change the way everything appears. For this reason, we think they are better labeled "interpretive paradigms," not scientific hypotheses.

People tend to embrace a position on Origins for the wrong reasons. They might accept the opinions of a respected scholar or pastor, or the first explanation they heard, or the position thought to be the least controversial.

Once people embrace a position, they then organize, evaluate, and interpret relevant observations and arguments according to their chosen paradigm. Thus YEC, OEC, EC, DE, and AE all organize, evaluate, and interpret the same data to fit their positions. And since most of the questions of Origins cannot be answered with a high degree of certainty, people in every camp find their paradigm validated by any new data, evidence, or argument.

The disadvantage of this strategy is that it does not allow for a person to change his or her position as new data and evidence are discovered. Whatever position you adopt, you should hold it tentatively (since the evidence is not overwhelmingly decisive for any of the positions).

Ultimately, accepting any creation position is a faith statement. The writer of Hebrews said it like this: "By faith we understand that the universe was formed at God's command, so that what is seen was not made out of what was visible" (Heb 11:3, NIV).

In the same way, accepting any other position on Origins is also a faith statement. For example, embracing macroevolution is a faith statement; faith is placed in the scientific method and human reasoning to discover what happened a very long time ago.

As a Christian, you do not have to reach a definite conclusion on all of the questions of Origins. Recognizing God as Creator is very important in the spiritual life of Christians. But we should also recognize that the Bible does not answer all of our questions about how or when the Creator created.

Bible-believing, Spirit-filled, spiritually mature, dynamic Christians can be Old Earth Creationists, Young Earth Creationists, or Evolutionary Creationists. Since none of these groups is likely to win the Origins debate any time soon, we should seek as much common ground as possible and accept each other to present a united witness to the world.

Ralph Winter said it well: "We can totally disagree with someone else's interpretation of the Bible without accusing them of not believing the Bible itself."[42] About sixteen-hundred years ago, St. Augustine cautioned believers to integrate different kinds of knowledge when he wrote:

Usually, even a non-Christian knows something about the earth, the heavens, and the other elements of this world, about the motion and orbit of the stars and even their size and relative positions, about the predictable eclipses of the sun and moon, the cycles of the years and the seasons, about the kinds of animals, shrubs, stones, and so forth, and this knowledge he holds to as being certain from reason and experience.

Now, it is a disgraceful and dangerous thing for an infidel to hear a Christian, presumably giving the meaning of Holy Scripture, talking nonsense on these topics; and we should take all means to prevent such an embarrassing situation, in which people show up vast ignorance in a Christian and laugh it to scorn.

The shame is not so much that an ignorant individual is derided, but that people outside the household of the faith think our sacred writers held such opinions, and, to the great loss of those for whose salvation we toil, the writers of our Scripture are criticized and rejected as unlearned men.

If they find a Christian mistaken in a field which they themselves know well and hear him maintaining his foolish opinions about our books, how are

---

[42] *International Journal of Frontier Missions*, 20:4, Winter, 2003, (108).

they going to believe those books in matters concerning the resurrection of the dead, the hope of eternal life, and the kingdom of heaven, when they think their pages are full of falsehoods on facts which they themselves have learnt from experience and the light of reason?

Reckless and incompetent expounders of Holy Scripture bring untold trouble and sorrow on their wiser brethren when they are caught in one of their mischievous false opinions and are taken to task by those who are not bound by the authority of our sacred books.

For then, to defend their utterly foolish and obviously untrue statements, they will try to call upon Holy Scripture for proof and even recite from memory many passages which they think support their position, although they understand neither what they say nor the things about which they make assertion.[43]

---

[43] Augustine, *St. Augustine: The Literal Meaning of Genesis,* Vol. I, Books 1-6, Quasten and others, eds., translated and annotated by John Hammond Taylor, S. J. Ancient Christian Writers: The Works of the Fathers in Translation, No. 41, Newman Press, 1982, pp.42-43. We have separated each sentence into a single paragraph to improve readability. *Italics in the original.*

Appendix 1

Now that you have considered how you could integrate philosophy, natural science, and biblical interpretation to inform your conclusions about creation-evolution, you might locate your personal position on the graph provided below.

The GCA is ancient fiction like the other ANE creation myths.					
The GCA is neither historical narrative nor scientifically accurate.					
The GCA is historical narrative & reflects ancient Jewish understanding of nature (science).					
The GCA is historical narrative that is accurate in terms of modern science.					

Your view of the Genesis creation account

Your confidence in the methods of science
to answer the questions of Origins

Low confidence ⟵-----------⟶ High confidence

Appendix 2

Recommendations for Productive Dialogue

Discussions of Origins often produce more heat than light. On the basis of several decades of experience, we offer the following suggestions and resources to help equip you to discuss the issues of Origins constructively with those who agree or disagree with you.

- Identify your goals. What is your purpose in understanding and debating theories of Origins? Are you seeking "truth" or trying to win an argument? Have you honestly considered the arguments of your friend? Or have you considered only one side of the debate?

- Understand yourself before you try to understand your friend. Do you embrace your position because this is the only way to understand the evidence—or for other reasons?

- Don't misrepresent your friend's position by bringing up discarded arguments that are no longer used (e.g., fossilized human and dinosaur footprints in the same stratum).

- Don't make your position the litmus test for scientific orthodoxy or religious orthodoxy.

- Don't assume you know your friend's motive for embracing his/her position.

- Become familiar with the biblical and scientific evidences for the age of the universe/earth.

- Carefully evaluate the patterns of integrating faith and science.

- Don't relegate science and religion to two separate domains (NOMA).

- Don't think only Christians use faith and only scientists use reason. Both use both.

- Natural science can neither prove nor disprove God's existence.

Can people in different camps discuss theories of Origins productively? Or must we have only heated arguments? Creating genuine dialogue requires a strong desire on the part of both parties. In addition to the advice above, here are some more suggestions to help you discuss Origins with a friend who holds an opinion different from yours.

- Each of you must train yourself to listen. People often are trying to think of and remember what they will say next rather than really listening to the other person. Discipline yourself to listen to your friend the same way you want him/her to listen to you.

- Define your terms. Be sure that you both mean the same thing by a particular word. Is one of you using a popular definition and the other a technical one? How are people using these terms in the literature today (as opposed to 25 or 50 years ago)?

- Be willing to admit and reveal your presuppositions, both to yourself and to your friend. Then use this knowledge in your discussion. If you are a Christian who considers the Bible to be God's Word and your friend doubts God's existence and has no respect for the Bible, you are not likely to convince that person by citing Genesis.

- Help your friend identify his/her presuppositions. If you embrace a creation theory and your friend thinks the scientific method is the only way to gain reliable knowledge about Origins, you will need to discover scientific challenges to the theory of macroevolution. If you are scientifically illiterate, your friend will probably not listen to your arguments for long.

- Discuss the merits of evidence and conclusions instead of attacking the other person. Even if you think people in other camps are less informed, less intelligent, or less spiritual than you, don't talk or act like it.

- Educate yourself. Read articles and books by those who hold opinions different from yours. Try to discover their presuppositions and any agenda they may have. (Everyone who writes has a bias and an agenda.)

- If in the end neither of you can convince the other of his/her position, admit that you have this difference of opinion and learn to accept each other—especially if you are both Christians.

- Many genuine Christians who agree that the Bible is God's Holy Word disagree on the genre of the creation account in Genesis. Your position should not be the litmus test for orthodoxy.

- Many orthodox Christians believe there is considerable empirical evidence that the universe is billions of years old.

- Accepting an ancient creation does not mean that you accept macroevolution.

- The theory of macroevolution is not "known" in the same way that the speed of light in a vacuum is "known." Some highly respected scientists today admit to problems with macroevolutionary theory.

- Scientific methods are not the only way to gain reliable knowledge and cannot find the answer to every question or the solution to every problem.

- The fact that a large percentage of natural scientists accept macroevolution may say more about our methods of education than it says about the merits of the theory or the amount of supporting evidence.

- Finally, those of us who teach need to remember that good teachers try to let the evidences speak for themselves. We suggest that teachers should present evidences for the various theories of Origins along with the unavoidable uncertainty of the scientific method, the unavoidable effect of worldview on data interpretation, and the alternative theist explanations. Show students the options, and give them the freedom to think and arrive at their own conclusions.

Sources and Resources

Below is a list of materials that describe either the interface between the natural sciences and Christian faith or the creation-evolution debate. This is not intended to constitute an endorsement of any work. Some of these are cited in our endnotes.

TOP TEN: (These are arranged alphabetically by the first author's last name.) If you read nothing else, read these!

1. Behe, Michael J. *Darwin's Black Box: The Biochemical Challenge to Evolution.* Free Press, 1996.
2. Behe, Michael J. *The Edge of Evolution: The Search for the Limits of Darwinism.* Free Press, 2007.
3. Bube, Richard. *Putting It All Together: Seven Patterns for Relating Science and the Christian Faith.* University Press of America, 1995.
4. Collins, C. John. *Genesis 1-4: A Linguistic, Literary, and Theological Commentary.* P&R, 2006.
5. Glover, Gordon. *Beyond the Firmament.* Chesapeake: Watertree Press, 2007.
6. Lamoureux, Denis. *I Love Jesus and I Accept Evolution.* Wipf & Stock, 2009.
7. Moreland, J. P. and John Mark Reynolds. *Three Views on Creation and Evolution.* Zondervan, 1999.
8. Ross, Hugh. *Creation and Time: A Biblical and Scientific Perspective on the Creation-Date Controversy,* NavPress, 1994.
9. Walton, John. *The Lost World of Genesis One: Ancient Cosmology and the Origins Debate.* IVP, 2009.
10. Whorton, Mark and Hill Roberts. *Holman QuickSource Guide to Understanding Creation.* B&H Publishing, 2008.

Age of Creation

Ross, Hugh. *Creation and Time: A Biblical and Scientific Perspective on the Creation-Date Controversy*. NavPress, 1994.

Young, Davis A. *Christianity and the Age of the Earth*. Zondervan, 1982.

Creation and Evolution

Glover, Gordon. *Beyond the Firmament*. Chesapeake: Watertree Press, 2007.

Hunter, Cornelius. *Darwin's God: Evolution and the Problem of Evil*. Brazos Press, 2001.

Johnson, Phillip and Denis Lamoureaux. *Darwinism Defeated? The Johnson-Lamoureux Debate on Biological Origins*. Regent College, 1999.

Johnson, Phillip. *Darwin on Trial*, 2nd ed. IVP, 1993.

Meyer, S.C. and M. N. Keas, "The meanings of evolution" in *Darwinism, Design, and Public Education* eds. John A. Campbell and Stephen C. Meyer, (Rhetoric and Public Affairs Series), Michigan State University Press, 2003.

Thurman, Duane. *How to Think About Evolution and Other Bible-Science Controversies*. IVP, 1978.

Van Till, Howard J., Davis Young, and Clarence Menninga. *Science Held Hostage: What's Wrong with Creation Science and Evolutionism*. IVP, 1988.

Wells, Jonathan. *Icons of Evolution: Why Much of What We Teach about Evolution Is Wrong*. Regnery, 2000.

Wright, Richard T. *Biology through the Eyes of Faith*, Revised and Expanded Edition. HarperSanFrancisco, 2003.

Integration of Christianity and the Natural Sciences

Barbour, Ian. *Religion in an Age of Science*. San Francisco: Harper & Row, 1990.

Barr, Stephen M. *Modern Physics and Ancient Faith*. Notre Dame: Notre Dame Press, 2003.

Bube, Richard. Putting It All Together: Seven Patterns for Relating Science and the Christian Faith. University Press of America, 1995.

Carlson, Richard F. *Science & Christianity: Four Views*. IVP, 2000.

Collins, Francis S. *The Language of God: A Scientist Presents Evidence for Belief*. Free Press, 2006.

Falk, Darrel R. *Coming to Peace with Science: Bridging the Worlds between Faith and Biology*. Downers Grove: InterVarsity Press, 2004.

Gregersen, Niels Henrik and J. Wentzel Van Huyssteen, eds. *Rethinking Theology and Science: Six Models for the Current Dialogue*. Grand Rapids: Eerdmans Publishing, 1998.

Henry, Granville C. *Christianity and the Images of Science.* Macon, Smyth and Helwys Publishing, 1998.

Waltke, Bruce K. "The Literary Genre of Genesis, Chapter One." *Crux* 27 (December 1991) 2-10.

Intelligent Design and a Finely-Tuned Universe

Barrow, John D., Frank Tipler, and John Wheeler. *The Anthropic Cosmological Principle.* Oxford University Press, 1988.

Behe, Michael J. *Darwin's Black Box: The Biochemical Challenge to Evolution.* Free Press, 1996.

Behe, Michael J., William A. Dembski, Stephen C. Meyer. *Science and Evidence for Design in the Universe.* Papers presented at a conference sponsored by the Wethersfield Institute, New York City, September 25, 1999. Ignatius Press, 2000.

Dembski William A. and Charles W. Colson. *The Design Revolution: Answering the Toughest Questions about Intelligent Design.* IVP, 2004.

Dembski, William A. ed. *Mere Creation: Science, Faith & Intelligent Design.* IVP, 1998.

Dembski, William A. *Intelligent Design: The Bridge between Science & Theology.* IVP, 1999.

Gonzalez, Guillermo and Jay W. Richards. *The Privileged Planet: How Our Place in the Cosmos Is Designed for Discovery.* Regnery Publishers, Lanham, 2004.

Meyer, Stephen C. *Signature in the Cell: DNA and the Evidence for Intelligent Design.* HarperOne, 2009.

Moreland, J.P. *The Creation Hypothesis: Scientific Evidence for an Intelligent Designer.* IVP, 1994.

Ward, Peter D. and Donald Brownlee. *Rare Earth: Why Complex Life Is Uncommon in the Universe.* Copernicus, 2003.

Witham, Larry. *By Design: Science and the Search for God.* Encounter Books, 2003.

Origins Positions

Assemblies of God Position Paper: "The Doctrine of Creation." Available online   at http://ag.org/top/Beliefs/Position_Papers/pp_downloads/PP_The_Doctrine_of_Creation.pdf, 2010.

Hagopian, David, ed. The Genesis Debate: Three Views on the Days of Creation. Crux Press, 2001.

Lamoureux, Denis. *I Love Jesus and I Accept Evolution.* Wipf & Stock, 2009.

_____. Evolutionary Creation: A Christian Approach to Evolution. Wipf & Stock, 2008.

Moreland, J.P. and John Mark Reynolds. *Three Views on Creation and Evolution.* Zondervan, 1999.

Ramm, Bernard. The Christian View of Science and Scripture. Eerdmans. 1954.

Ross, Hugh. *The Fingerprint of God,* 2nd ed. Promise Pub., 1991.

Sarfati, Jonathan. *Refuting Compromise: A Biblical and Scientific Refutation of 'Progressive Creationism' (Billions of Years), As Popularized by Astronomer Hugh Ross.* Master Books, 2004.

Whitcomb, John and HenryMorris. *The Genesis Flood; The Biblical Rrecord and Its Scientific Implications.* Presbyterian and Reformed Publishers, 1961.

Wise, Kurt. *Faith, Form, and Time: What the Bible Teaches and Science Confirms about Creation and the Age of the Universe.* Broadman & Holman, 2002.

Philosophy of Science

Brush, Nigel. *The Limitations of Scientific Truth.* Kregel, 2005.

Godfrey-Smith, Peter. Theory and Reality: *An Introduction to the Philosophy of Science.* University of Chicago Press, 2003.

Kuhn, Thomas. *The Structure of Scientific Revolutions,* 2nd ed. University of Chicago Press, 1970.

Moreland, J.P. and William Lane Craig. *Philosophical Foundations for a Christian Worldview.* Intervarsity Press, 2003.

Moreland, J.P. *Christianity and the Nature of Science: A Philosophical Investigation.* Baker, 1989.

Pearcey, Nancy and Charles Thaxton. *The Soul of Science: Christian Faith and Natural Philosophy.* Crossway Books, 1994.

Pearcey, Nancy. *Total Truth: Liberating Christianity from Its Cultural Captivity.* Crossway, 2004.

Ratzsch, Del. *Philosophy of Science: The Natural Sciences in Christian Perspective.* IVP, 1986.

Religion-Science Dialogue

Banner, Michael C. *The Justification of Science and the Rationality of Religious Belief.* Oxford University Press, 1990.

McGrath, Alister. *Science and Religion: An Introduction.* London: Blackwell Publishers, 1999.

McGrath, Alister. *The Foundations of Dialogue in Science and Religion.* London: Blackwell Publishers, 1998.

Poythress, Vern. *Science and Hermeneutics.* Zondervan, 1988.

Ruse, Michael. *Can a Darwinian Be A Christian? The Relationship Between Science and Religion.* Cambridge University Press, 2001.

Watts, Fraser and Kevin Dutton, eds. *Why the Science and Religion Dialogue Matters.* Philadelphia: Templeton Foundation Press, 2006.

Weaver, John. *In the Beginning God: Modern Science and the Christian Doctrine of Creation.* Regent's Park College, 1994.

Internet Resources

www.answersingenesis.org/

Dedicated to helping Christians defend their faith and proclaim the gospel of Jesus Christ effectively, Answers in Genesis focuses on providing answers to questions about the Bible—particularly the book of Genesis—regarding key issues such as creation, evolution, science, and the age of the earth.

www.reasons.org

Reasons To Believe is a progressive creationist ministry that promotes day-age forms of old Earth creationism. It was founded in 1986 by Hugh Ross, a Canadian-born astrophysicist and creationist Christian apologist.

www.biologos.org

BioLogos invites the church and the world to see the harmony between science and biblical faith as we present an evolutionary understanding of God's creation.

www.asa3.org/

This has an excellent collection of Christian thinking on Origins (primarily from an OEC or a EC perspective) covering the past several decades. Many full text articles are available in their online archives of *Perspectives on Science and Christian Faith* (the Journal of the American Scientific Affiliation).

www.arn.org/

"We focus on such controversial topics as genetic engineering, euthanasia, computer technology, environmental issues, creation/evolution, fetal tissue research, AIDS, and so on." One main focus is on Intelligent Design.

http://www.discovery.org/

The "discovery institute's mission is to make a positive vision of the future practical. the institute discovers and promotes ideas in the common sense tradition of representative government, the free market and individual liberty.

our mission is promoted through books, reports, legislative testimony, articles, public conferences and debates, plus media coverage and the institute's own publications. current projects explore the fields of technology, science and culture, reform of the law, national defense, the environment and the economy, the future of democratic institutions, transportation, religion and public life, government entitlement spending, foreign affairs."

www.icr.org/

This site provides an abundance of information promoting the Young Earth Creationist perspective.

www.natcenscied.org/

The goal of this organization is to keep evolution in public school education. There is a lot of useful information here from a materialistic perspective dealing with evolution and creation.

www.talkorigins.org/

This is a Usenet newsgroup that discusses a wide range of viewpoints and evidences related to biological and physical origins.

http://www.pctii.org/cyberj/cyberj20/tenneson_badger.html

The authors each describe the faith journeys that led them to their positions on Origins and to write this booklet.

http://home.entouch.net/dmd/gstory.htm

Christian geologist Glenn R. Morton shares his personal struggles with both faith, science, and his attempt to integrate the two. Very interesting reading.

About the Authors

Dr. Steve Badger, professor emeritus, began teaching chemistry at Evangel University in 2001. He has earned degrees in chemistry (PhD) and biology (BS). He has been involved in scientific research in both government and private research laboratories. He is ordained with the Assemblies of God and has served as both senior pastor and associate pastor. His master's degree in biblical literature from the Assemblies of God Theological Seminary also allows him to teach Bible courses both at home and abroad. He and his wife have two daughters and two grand-daughters. The Badger family also shares a passion for Thai food. Steve and co-author Mike Tenneson have been researching Christians' attitudes and beliefs about Origins for over twelve years.

Mike Tenneson, professor of biology, has taught at Evangel University for more than 25 years. He earned a Ph.D. from the University of Missouri in science education, master's degrees in biology/statistics (University North Dakota) and missiology/biblical literature (Assemblies of God Theological Seminary), and a bachelor's degree in biology from University of California, Los Angeles. Mike has been involved in research related to the faith/science interface for many years and has authored or co-authored numerous book chapters, articles and presentations on faith and science topics. He has done field research on bird incubation behavior, frog mating systems, porcupine ecology, lizard distribution and ecology, and tropical snail distribution. He is married to a biologist, Cheryl, and they have three children.

Online Origins Survey

The authors have developed a survey designed to measure a person's opinions about faith and science. The survey is taken online, and the results are easily analyzed.

If you are interested in using this survey with your classes (or other group), contact Mike Tenneson or Steve Badger.

Mike Tenneson: tennesonm@evangel.edu
Steve Badger: docbadger@gmail.com

Evangel University
1111 North Glenstone Avenue
Springfield, Missouri 65802
417.865.2815
www.evangel.edu

CPSIA information can be obtained
at www.ICGtesting.com
Printed in the USA
BVHW041229181218
535877BV00020B/3920/P